TAKING A STAND

SOPHIE SCHOLL
FIGHTS HITLER'S REGIME

by Clara MacCarald

FOCUS READERS

www.focusreaders.com

Focus Readers is distributed by North Star Editions:
sales@northstareditions.com | 888-417-0195

Produced for Focus Readers by Red Line Editorial.

Content Consultant: Edward Snyder, Associate Professor of History, Chowan University

Photographs ©: George (Jürgen) Wittenstein/AKG-images, cover, 1; -/picture-alliance/dpa/AP Images, 4–5; Splash News/Newscom, 7; Everett Historical/Shutterstock Images, 8–9, 13, 14–15, 27, 28–29, 31; AP Images, 10; Red Line Editorial, 16, 40; Authenticated News/Archive Photos/Getty Images, 19; Photo12/Archives Snark/Alamy, 21; akg-images/Newscom, 22–23; forma82/Shutterstock Images, 25; Interfoto/Alamy, 33, 35; Peter Kneffel/dpa/picture-alliance/Newscom, 36–37; Clemens Bilan/dapd/AP Images, 39; Heinz-Jürgen Göttert/picture-alliance/dpa/AP Images, 42–43; anahtiris/Shutterstock Images, 45

Library of Congress Cataloging-in-Publication Data
Names: MacCarald, Clara, 1979- author.
Title: Sophie Scholl fights Hitler's regime / by Clara MacCarald.
Description: Lake Elmo, MN : Focus Readers, [2019] | Series: Taking a stand |
   Includes index. | Audience: Grades 7-8.
Identifiers: LCCN 2018037881 (print) | LCCN 2018041372 (ebook) | ISBN
   9781641855327 (PDF) | ISBN 9781641854740 (e-book) | ISBN 9781641853583
   (hardcover) | ISBN 9781641854160 (pbk.)
Subjects: LCSH: Scholl, Sophie, 1921-1943--Juvenile literature. |
   Germany--History--1933-1945--Juvenile literature. | CYAC: White Rose
   (German resistance group)--Juvenile literature.
Classification: LCC DD256.3 (ebook) | LCC DD256.3 .M227 2019 (print) | DDC
   940.53/43092 [B] --dc23
LC record available at https://lccn.loc.gov/2018037881

Printed in the United States of America
Mankato, MN
October, 2018

ABOUT THE AUTHOR

Clara MacCarald is a freelance writer with a master's degree in biology. She lives with her family in an off-grid house nestled in the forests of central New York. When not parenting her daughter, she spends her time writing nonfiction books for kids.

TABLE OF CONTENTS

CHAPTER 1

RISKING ALL

On February 18, 1943, Sophie Scholl and her older brother Hans entered the University of Munich in Germany. They headed for the university's main building. Although Sophie and Hans were students, they weren't going to class. Hans carried a suitcase. If they got caught, its contents could get them both killed.

The suitcase was filled with leaflets, or flyers, calling students to rise up against the Nazi Party.

Sophie Scholl was a teenager during the rise of Nazi Germany.

This political party controlled the German government as a **dictatorship**. Anyone who tried to resist the Nazis risked arrest. In fact, the Nazi **secret police**, or Gestapo, were already looking for the people who were making the leaflets.

The Scholls and their friends had created the leaflets. They had heard stories of the Nazis killing hundreds of thousands of people. And they had seen Nazis treat Jewish people horribly. Despite the danger of resistance, they felt the need to speak out.

At the university, students were attending classes. Sophie and Hans knew they had to work fast. They placed piles of leaflets in front of doors, on windowsills, and along staircases. As the classes ended, the siblings had only a small pile of leaflets left. Sophie hurried to the top level of the building. She tossed the leaflets over an open

▲ This scene from the film *Sophie Scholl: The Final Days* shows Sophie and Hans' leaflets floating to the ground.

area at the building's center. Paper rained down on the students below as they left their classes.

Sophie and Hans turned to leave. Suddenly, one of the school's janitors appeared. He had seen Sophie and Hans distributing the leaflets. They tried to blend in with the other students, but the janitor caught them. He turned them over to the Gestapo.

CHAPTER 2

DARK CLOUDS OVER EUROPE

Sophie Scholl was born in 1921 in a small town in southern Germany. The Scholls moved to the city of Ulm when Sophie was 11 years old. In January 1933, Adolf Hitler became the German **chancellor**. Hitler led the Nazi Party. He used his new position to begin taking over the German government. At the end of February, his **regime** passed a law that took away the **civil rights** of German citizens.

Adolf Hitler waves to crowds during a parade.

△ Members of the female branch of the Hitler Youth celebrate in Berlin after the Nazis take power in 1933.

Hitler talked about returning Germany to former greatness. He promised to bring its people happiness and freedom. At first, many Germans believed him. They included the Scholl children. Like many of their peers, Sophie and her siblings joined a group called the Hitler Youth. Members wore uniforms, marched together, and supported the Nazi regime. They even spied on their parents for signs of disloyalty to the Nazis.

Sophie's father did not want his children to join this group. He was horrified by the Nazis. At first, Sophie and her siblings disagreed. They found the group exciting. Later, however, they began to have doubts. Although Sophie enjoyed the group's camping trips, she wondered why her Jewish friends couldn't join. And Hans grew disgusted by the hateful speech Nazi leaders used. As the Scholl children learned more about the Nazis, they came to agree with their father.

Hans left the Hitler Youth in 1936. That year, the Nazis banned all other youth organizations. However, many groups continued to operate in secret. Some groups even took direct action against the Nazis. For a short time, Hans led a group that opposed the Nazis' political ideas. The members shared songs and writings that the Nazis had banned.

Soon, though, other responsibilities distracted Hans. He needed to complete his national service. Germany required all men between the ages of 18 and 25 to spend six months working for the National Labor Service. Hans spent his time building a highway. Afterward, the law required him to serve two years in the military. The military sent Hans to a base near Ulm.

Meanwhile, the Scholls joined a secret reading circle of people who opposed Hitler. Group members sent one another writings banned by the Nazis. They also wrote essays that criticized the regime. Sophie and her sister even created a newsletter. They tried to be subtle about their opposition in case the wrong person found the paper.

Unfortunately, officials caught on. In 1937, the Gestapo arrived at Sophie's house. Sophie's

The National Labor Service required workers to do physical labor.

mother managed to remove illegal items from the house. But officers took nearly the whole family in for questioning. The Gestapo even sent officers to the military base where Hans was stationed.

Sophie was released later that day. But Hans wasn't freed for three weeks. Sophie knew the Gestapo could return at any time. And the next time, her family might not be as lucky.

CHAPTER 3

A NATION AT WAR

Sophie's life took another turn in 1939. On September 1, Germany invaded Poland. Hitler believed the German people needed *Lebensraum*, which means "living space." He wanted to gain land so Germany could expand. Hitler's invasion of Poland marked the beginning of World War II (1939–1945). Hans was studying medicine at the University of Munich. In May 1940, the government sent him to France as a **medic**.

A German airplane flies over Poland in 1939.

Back in Germany, the government pressured people to support the war effort. But Sophie was against the war. She saw the Nazis as a threat to her country and to human freedom. She had heard stories of their cruelty.

➤ GERMAN FORCES SWEEP THROUGH EUROPE (1942)

Germany, allies, and occupied zones | Allies opposing Germany | Neutral countries

For example, a family friend worked with children with disabilities. One day, the Nazis gathered the children into trucks. The friend knew the Nazis planned to kill the children. But there was nothing she could do. The Nazis would eventually kill hundreds of thousands of people with disabilities. Public protests broke out. But the Nazis only worked harder to hide their actions.

Hans returned from France and continued his studies in April 1941. Sophie planned to go to college, too. But she still had to work six months for the National Labor Service. The government sent her to do farmwork. She lived in a cold, damp castle with a group of other girls. Sophie was finally able to attend college in 1942. She joined her brother at the University of Munich.

One day, Sophie found a leaflet under a desk. It was signed by a group called the White Rose.

The leaflet accused the Nazis of horrible crimes. It encouraged German people to resist the party. At the end, it asked readers to make copies of the leaflet and spread its message to other people.

In Nazi Germany, citizens had to report any materials that spoke out against the government. Many university students supported the Nazis. But Sophie wanted to know more about the people who dared to write such dangerous things. She decided to show the leaflet to her brother.

Sophie and Hans shared an apartment. While Sophie waited for Hans at home, she discovered something in his room. The leaflet quoted a book

➤ THINK ABOUT IT

When Sophie chose not to report the leaflet, she was breaking the law. Do you think breaking the law is ever acceptable? Why or why not?

⚠ Hans and Sophie Scholl became part of the resistance movement in Nazi Germany.

Hans owned. And inside his copy, someone had underlined the exact words from the leaflet.

When Hans returned, Sophie confronted him. At first, Hans refused to tell her anything. But Sophie wouldn't back down. Finally, Hans admitted that he and his friends had created the leaflets. They wanted to inspire people to stand up to the Nazi regime.

SOPHIE SCHOLL

During the summer of 1940, Sophie wrote letters to her boyfriend, Fritz Hartnagel. Fritz had joined the air force, despite Sophie's urging him to stay out of the war. In her letters, Sophie continued to share her concerns. "It isn't easy to banish all thoughts of the war," Sophie wrote. "And I could weep at how mean people are . . . and how they betray their fellow creatures. Isn't it enough to make a person lose heart sometimes?"

Sophie didn't want to give in to the Nazis. "All that matters fundamentally," Sophie wrote, "is whether we come through, whether we manage to hold our own among the majority, whose sole concern is self-interest—those who approve of any means to their own ends." The White Rose hadn't yet formed, but Sophie was ready to stand up for what was right.

⬆ Sophie learned more about the war through Fritz's letters.

"Dear Fritz, this whole letter will probably strike you as odd in the extreme," she wrote. Fritz believed in the honor of being a soldier, even if he was fighting for the Nazis. Eventually, Sophie's letters would change his mind about the Nazis.

Hans Scholl and Sophie Scholl. *At the Heart of the White Rose: Letters and Diaries of Hans and Sophie Scholl.* Walden, NY: Plough Publishing House, 2017. Print. 76.

CHAPTER 4

THE WHITE ROSE

During the summer of 1942, the White Rose created several different leaflets. Each leaflet covered the front and back of one sheet of paper. Hans and his friends wrote the leaflets on a typewriter. Then they used a duplicating machine to make nearly 100 copies.

Group members spread these copies across Munich. They mailed many leaflets to random houses. They left other leaflets in public places.

Actors playing Hans and Sophie Scholl distribute leaflets in the 1982 German film *The White Rose*.

Each leaflet criticized the Nazis and their actions. For example, one leaflet detailed the crimes Nazis had committed in Poland. It said the Nazis had sent Polish people to concentration camps. Hundreds of these prison-like camps existed throughout Europe.

The Nazis sent anyone they considered enemies to the camps. There, they forced prisoners to do hard labor. By the end of the war, the Nazis killed millions of Jewish people in camps made for mass murder. These were called death camps. The leaflet accused readers of knowing about the Nazis' crimes and doing nothing.

> ➤ THINK ABOUT IT

The White Rose wanted the German people to resist Hitler. Do you think people have a responsibility to stop injustice when they see it? Why or why not?

▲ Auschwitz was the Nazis' largest death and concentration camp complex.

The leaflets called for Germans to resist Hitler's regime. They encouraged people to destroy Nazi art. The Nazis used art to spread their message to the German people. The art praised Hitler and mocked Jewish people. The White Rose's leaflets also called for people to interfere with the war effort by **sabotaging** factories. Some leaflets even said Germans should try to overthrow Hitler's regime.

After Sophie found the leaflet, she joined the White Rose, too. She helped the group buy a second duplicating machine. She also helped create and spread the leaflets. The work was dangerous. Sometimes Sophie felt scared. But she loved her country and felt that she needed to stop its current government.

In July 1942, Hitler sent more than three million soldiers to take over the Soviet Union. The government forced Hans and his male friends to work as medics during their school break. The military sent them to the Eastern battle lines. While traveling, the students saw German soldiers treat Jewish people in horrible ways. They saw soldiers murder innocent people.

In October, Hans and his friends returned to Munich. The White Rose was more determined than ever to end Nazi rule. That fall, the members

△ German bombs caused significant damage to the Soviet city of Stalingrad.

wrote a new leaflet. This time, they created thousands of copies.

Once again, Sophie helped distribute copies. She was careful to avoid detection by the Gestapo. The secret police already suspected the leaflets came from students in Munich. Sophie bought small amounts of paper in several places rather than buying a large amount at once. She hoped that would look less suspicious. In addition, White Rose members traveled to other German cities to mail the leaflets. That way, the Gestapo would not know where the leaflets had been created.

CHAPTER 5

THE GESTAPO CLOSES IN

In early 1943, a Nazi official gave a speech to University of Munich students at a nearby museum. He told the female students they were wasting time by attending school. Instead, he said all women should get married and stay at home. Like Hitler, the official claimed the household was the natural place for women. There, they should support Germany by having a baby every year.

A 1942 Nazi poster encouraged Germans to support the war.

Angered by the official's comments, female students tried to walk out. Nazis arrested many of them. Both male and female students forced the Nazis to release the captives. They marched down the street toward the university, singing. The students broke up before the police could crush their protest. But Sophie felt hope. Maybe this small revolt would lead to a wider uprising.

On February 3, an announcement came over the radio. German troops had been destroyed in the Soviet city of Stalingrad. Soviets had captured or killed 330,000 German soldiers. This news shocked many Germans. German leaders had been telling the public that Germany was winning the war. But the announcement said otherwise.

Sophie and her friends seized the moment. They covered walls around Munich with **graffiti** of anti-Nazi sayings. At night, men from the White

△ Approximately 90,000 Germans were taken prisoner at the end of the Battle of Stalingrad.

Rose roamed the streets with buckets of paint. They painted anti-Nazi sayings on churches, office buildings, and even a military monument. They also drew crossed-out Nazi symbols. Some of the graffiti could not be washed off. Gestapo officers were furious.

Later that month, Sophie and Hans carried out another bold plan. On February 18, they left leaflets in the main building of their university.

They hoped students would find the leaflets between classes. But the school's janitor caught the Scholls as they tried to leave.

The janitor brought the Scholls and their suitcase to the Gestapo. At first, the Scholls denied everything. They said the suitcase was empty because Sophie was planning to take the train home and fill it with clean clothes. Sophie and Hans seemed so calm that the Gestapo almost believed them.

But Hans had a draft of another leaflet in his pocket. This leaflet hadn't been typed up yet. It was in the handwriting of Hans's friend Christopher Probst. Hans tried to eat it before the Gestapo searched him. The officers saw what he was doing and stopped him.

Hans said an unknown student had given him the paper. He claimed he was destroying

A Christopher Probst helped write and distribute the White Rose's leaflets.

it because he thought it looked suspicious. He swore he didn't know what it said. The officers were not convinced. They questioned each sibling separately. Meanwhile, other officers searched the Scholls' apartment. There, the Gestapo found a stash of stamps. Sophie and Hans were now in deep trouble.

KURT HUBER

Kurt Huber, a professor and White Rose member, wrote one of the leaflets. Germans had just learned about the defeat at Stalingrad. They felt overcome with grief. Many Germans felt Hitler had betrayed them. He had ordered the army to fight to the last man.

Huber put the public's rage and distress into words. "Fellow Fighters in the Resistance!" Huber wrote. "Shaken and broken, our people behold the loss of the men of Stalingrad." He said Hitler's strategy had led to death and destruction.

Huber wrote that university students should oppose the Nazi Party. "For us there is but one **slogan**: fight against the party!" According to Huber, only by opposing the regime could students regain their future.

Huber accused the Nazis of taking Germans' freedom. To him, freedom was "the most precious

▲ Kurt Huber was one of the few professors in Germany who resisted the Nazis.

treasure we have." In place of freedom, the Nazis had brought widespread slaughter to Europe. "The name of Germany is dishonored for all time if German youth does not finally rise," Huber wrote. "Students! The German people look to us."

"White Rose Leaflets." *Holocaust Research Project*. Holocaust Education and Archive Research Team, n.d. Web. 22 Aug. 2018.

CHAPTER 6

A FINAL RESISTANCE

Both Sophie and Hans were forced to confess. The siblings tried to protect their friends. They insisted no one else had taken part in their work. Hans even tried to convince the officers Sophie was innocent.

The officer questioning Sophie also tried to give her a way out. Because she was a girl, he believed she must not have given her actions full thought. If she blamed her brother, she could live.

White Rose members faced trial at the Palace of Justice. Today, a room there serves as a memorial.

But Sophie refused. She took full responsibility, even knowing she might die.

Officials gave Sophie a paper that charged her with treason. She looked outside, where people strolled in the sunshine. Then she wrote the word *freedom* on the paper. Her hands shook. Sophie stood by the White Rose's cause. If her actions had helped save others, she was willing to face death.

The trial took place on February 22. Sophie and Hans entered the court with Christopher Probst. The officers had identified Probst's handwriting in the leaflet. The judge raged and screamed, but the three friends remained strong. Sophie spoke up several times even though the judge tried to shout her down. She said they had done nothing wrong when they wrote the leaflets. They were only voicing what other people were afraid to say. The judge sentenced them all to death.

Im Namen
des Deutschen Volkes

47/ 43

In der Strafsache gegen
1.) den Hans Fritz S c h o l l aus München, geboren in Ingers-
heim am 22. September 1918,
2.) die Sophia Magdalena S c h o l l aus München, geboren in
...denberg am 9. Mai 1921,
...stoph Hermann P r o b s t aus Aldrans bei Inns-
...urnau am 6. November 1919,
...eser Sache in gerichtlicher Unt...

▲ This picture of a court record from the Scholls' trial was taken in front of a memorial at the Palace of Justice.

The Scholls' parents rushed to Munich when they heard the news. They were able to see their children one last time. Sophie smiled as she met her family, but she cried quietly when she returned to her cell.

A few hours after their trial, the guards fulfilled the sentences of Sophie, Hans, and Probst. Sophie did not falter on her way to execution. She stood for her beliefs until the very end.

Officials worried that students at the university would rise up when they learned of the executions.

Graffiti appeared on campus saying that "Scholl" still lived. Some students continued to spread leaflets. However, most students did nothing. Some felt it was their duty to support the Nazis. Others feared getting into trouble. After the Scholls' trial, the Gestapo rounded up other people involved with the White Rose. Most of the members received sentences of death or prison.

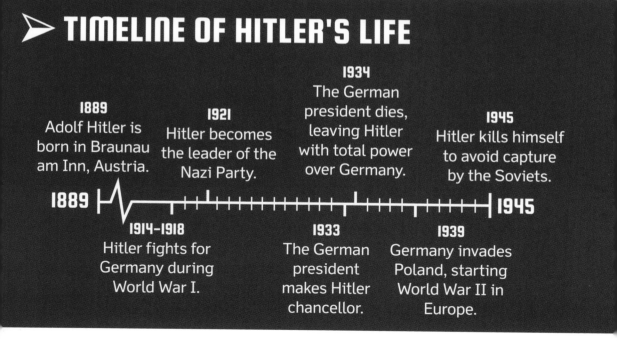

➤ TIMELINE OF HITLER'S LIFE

1889
Adolf Hitler is born in Braunau am Inn, Austria.

1921
Hitler becomes the leader of the Nazi Party.

1934
The German president dies, leaving Hitler with total power over Germany.

1945
Hitler kills himself to avoid capture by the Soviets.

1889 |—————————————————————————————| 1945

1914–1918
Hitler fights for Germany during World War I.

1933
The German president makes Hitler chancellor.

1939
Germany invades Poland, starting World War II in Europe.

News of the White Rose slowly spread. Newspapers around the world started reporting stories about the group. Eventually, one of the White Rose's leaflets reached the **Allied Forces**. This leaflet called for Germans to rise up for the sake of German soldiers lost at Stalingrad. Allied airplanes dropped millions of copies of it over German cities.

Germany was losing the war, but the Nazis refused to give up. Even after Hitler killed himself, Germans continued to fight. Soon, though, Berlin fell, and Germany surrendered to the Allies on May 7, 1945.

THINK ABOUT IT ◄

Why did the Allies drop copies of a White Rose leaflet on Germans? What might they have hoped would happen?

CHAPTER 7

LASTING IMPACT

By September 2, 1945, World War II had officially ended. However, Germans still faced the huge task of rebuilding their country. Millions of people had died, and bombs had laid whole cities to ruin. The Nazis had committed all kinds of **atrocities** while in power.

People in Germany and around the world were horrified by what the Nazis had done. The Nazi Party and its symbol became illegal in Germany.

In 1958, the University of Munich unveiled a new memorial in remembrance of the White Rose.

Some former Nazi officials faced trials for war crimes. The janitor who turned in the Scholls was also sent to jail.

The White Rose had given hope to Germans during the dark days of war. The families of the group's members did not want their bravery to fade away. They wrote about the memories of their loved ones and gave interviews about them.

Over time, many Germans celebrated the Scholls and their friends as heroes. They named streets and schools after members of the White Rose. Books and movies kept the group's story alive. The University of Munich also began holding a yearly talk in honor of the White Rose.

In 1990, an artist created a memorial at the entrance to the University of Munich. He set permanent leaflets into the sidewalk. They lay as a reminder of the courage of the White Rose.

▲ A memorial at the University of Munich recreated the leaflets as part of the sidewalk.

At a time when many Germans went along with the people in power, even when those people did terrible things, Sophie and her friends chose to take a stand. Their courageous actions continue to inspire people in Germany and around the world.

FOCUS ON
SOPHIE SCHOLL

Write your answers on a separate piece of paper.

1. Write a letter to a friend summarizing the main events of Chapter 4.

2. If you had been Sophie, would you have reported finding the leaflet to the authorities? Why or why not?

3. In what year did Hitler and the Nazi Party seize control of Germany?

> **A.** 1921
> **B.** 1933
> **C.** 1945

4. Why did the White Rose mail leaflets to random people instead of people they knew?

> **A.** They didn't want to give the Gestapo any clues about who was writing the leaflets.
> **B.** They already had enough support in Munich and wanted to focus on other areas.
> **C.** All the people they knew had already joined the army and were fighting overseas.

Answer key on page 48.

GLOSSARY

Allied Forces
The victorious countries of World War II, including the Soviet Union, the United Kingdom, France, and the United States.

atrocities
Extremely terrible or cruel crimes.

chancellor
The chief minister of some countries, such as Germany.

civil rights
Rights that protect people's freedom and equality.

dictatorship
A form of government in which one leader has absolute power.

graffiti
Writings or drawings on public surfaces such as walls.

medic
A person in the military who gives medical aid.

regime
A government, especially one that tightly controls its people.

sabotaging
Destroying things on purpose, especially to stop something from happening.

secret police
A police force that enforces a government's policies, typically through spying on citizens.

slogan
A saying that represents a group's goals or beliefs.

TO LEARN MORE

BOOKS

Murray, Hallie, and Ann Byers. *Teenage Resistance to the Nazi Regime.* New York: Enslow Publishing, 2018.

Roberts, Russell. *World War II Leaders.* Minneapolis: Abdo Publishing, 2016.

Voices from the Second World War: Stories of War as Told to Children of Today. Somerville, MA: Candlewick Press, 2018.

NOTE TO EDUCATORS

Visit **www.focusreaders.com** to find lesson plans, activities, links, and other resources related to this title.

INDEX

Answer Key: 1. Answers will vary; **2.** Answers will vary; **3.** B; **4.** A